Adorable Animals

Baby Gorillas

JUSTIN ERIC RUSSELL

BLACK RABBIT BOOKS

Bolt is published by Black Rabbit Books
P.O. Box 227, Mankato, Minnesota, 56002.
www.blackrabbitbooks.com

Marysa Storm, editor; Catherine Cates, interior designer; Grant Gould, cover designer; Omay Ayres, photo researcher

Library of Congress Cataloging-in-Publication Data
Names: Russell, Justin Eric, author.
Title: Baby gorillas / by Justin Eric Russell.
Description: Mankato, Minnesota : Black Rabbit Books, [2020] |
Series: Bolt. Adorable animals | Audience: Age 8-12. | Audience: Grade 4 to 6. |
Includes bibliographical references and index.
Identifiers: LCCN 2018025809 (print) | LCCN 2018028350 (ebook) |
ISBN 9781680727791 (e-book) | ISBN 9781680727715 (library binding) |
ISBN 9781644660027 (paperback)
Subjects: LCSH: Gorilla–Infancy–Juvenile literature.
Classification: LCC QL737.P94 (ebook) | LCC QL737.P94 R87 2020 (print) |
DDC 599.884–dc23
LC record available at https://lccn.loc.gov/2018025809

Image Credits

Alamy: Andrew Michael, 10–11; FLPA, 13, 29 (top); Top-Pics TBK, 18–19; Dreamstime: Lantapix, 26 (newborn); iStock: guenterguni, Cover; Pimpay, 14–15; Newscom: Schmidt Hendrik/DPA/ABACA, 22 (gorilla); Shutterstock: Angel DiBilio, 21; BEJITA, 22 (insect); Eric Gevaert, 7; fotoearl, 22 (thistle); Grant Tiffen, 3; GUDKOV ANDREY, 9; Ivanov Gleb, 1; Joseph Wright, 29 (btm); Karel Bartik, 26 (main); Kiki Dohmeier, 4–5, 8; natalia del rio galvan, 31; oorka, 26 (female), 27; Palii Oleg, 22 (bark); RudiErnst, 32; Ryan M. Bolton, 22 (fur); Simon Eeman, 16; uzuri, 24–25; Valentine Razumova, 22 (bamboo); Volosina, 22 (fruit)

Every effort has been made to contact copyright holders for material reproduced in this book. Any omissions will be rectified in subsequent printings if notice is given to the publisher.

Contents

CHAPTER 1

A Cute and Playful BABY

Two young gorillas wrestle on the jungle floor. The small, black fuzz balls tumble and roll. They chase each other around tall trees. Using strong arms, they climb up the branches. The two look out from the leafy trees with bright eyes. What a big green world it is!

Hold on Tight

Young gorillas are playful. But babies aren't ready to play right away. First, they must spend months at their mothers' sides.

Newborn gorillas arrive throughout the year. Mother gorillas hold their tiny babies to their chests. The little gorillas hang on tight. Babies are carried until they're four months old. Then they ride on their mothers' backs.

How Much Does a Newborn Gorilla Weigh?

Learning to Walk

Baby gorillas learn to crawl and walk quickly. By about two months old, they start crawling along the forest floor. At six to eight months old, gorillas begin walking. They can follow their mothers for short distances. They still ride on their mothers' backs when traveling, though. Young gorillas ride until they're about three years old.

BABY GORILLA FEATURES

LONG ARMS

CHAPTER 2

A Place to Call Home

Gorillas live in Africa's forests. They sleep, eat, and play in groups called troops. Troops usually have five to 30 gorillas. A strong male, called a silverback, leads each troop.

Troops travel often. The silverback decides where the group eats and sleeps. It makes sure the troop is safe and fed.

Silverbacks get their name from the silver hair on their backs.

GORILLA RANGE MAP

Gorillas never use the same nest twice.

Nests

When not eating or playing, gorillas sleep and rest in nests. Smaller gorillas can nest in trees. Heavier gorillas nest on the ground. Gorillas make their nests from leaves and branches. Mother gorillas share their nests with their young.

Playtime

Young gorillas learn by watching adults. They also learn by playing. Adults wrestle with them. Young gorillas play fight and chase each other. These actions let them practice physical **skills**. They also help them form **relationships**.

Gorillas touch noses when greeting each other.

CHAPTER 3

WHAT'S FOR DINNER?

Baby gorillas are born toothless. They can't eat solid food. So they drink their mothers' milk. Baby gorillas soon get their baby teeth. By about six months old, they are trying solid foods.

Adult male gorillas can eat up to 45 pounds (20 kg) of food each day.

Gorillas eat many different things.

thistles

bamboo

fruit

bark

insects

Favorite Foods

Fruit and bamboo quickly become some of young gorillas' favorite meals. Gorillas enjoy thistles and insects too. Young gorillas still **nurse**, though. They won't eat only solids until they're about three years old.

By THE NUMBERS

ABOUT EVERY
4½ years
HOW OFTEN FEMALES GIVE BIRTH

about
700

NUMBER OF MOUNTAIN GORILLAS IN THE WILD

1

NUMBER OF YOUNG FEMALES HAVE AT A TIME

35

YEARS

AVERAGE LIFE SPAN IN THE WILD

8½ MONTHS

how long female gorillas are **pregnant**

COMPARING WEIGHTS
NEWBORN
ADULT FEMALE
4 to 5 POUNDS (1.8 to 2.3 kg)
150 to 200 POUNDS (68 to 91 kg)

CHAPTER 4

Growing Up

After about three years riding on their mothers' backs, gorillas are **independent**. They quit drinking milk. They eat only solid foods. These gorillas make and sleep in their own nests too. They've learned how to make them by watching their mothers.

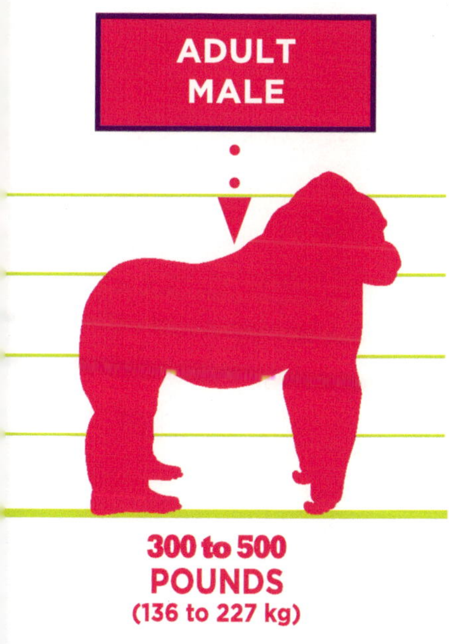

A Lot to Learn

Gorillas grow a lot in their first few years. But it takes a while until they're fully grown. At about eight years old, they leave their troops. Some females find new groups. Others find males to start their own troops with. Males often live alone for a while. But until then, there's a lot of learning left to do.

While walking, gorillas support their bodies with their knuckles. This way of moving is called knuckle walking.

independent (in-di-PEN-duhnt)—not relying on anyone or anything else

nurse (NURS)—to drink milk from the mother's body

pregnant (PREG-nuhnt)—carrying one or more unborn offspring in the body

relationship (ri-LEY-shuhn-ship)—the way in which two or more people or animals are connected

skill (SKIL)—the ability to do something that comes from training, experience, or practice

thistle (THIS-uhl)—a wild plant that has sharp points on its leaves

LEARN MORE

BOOKS

Caravan, Jill M. *Gorillas*. Animals in the Wild. Broomall, PA: Mason Crest, 2019.

Gagne, Tammy. *Gorillas*. Animals of Africa. Mankato, MN: Focus Readers, 2018.

Jones, Elton. *Gorillas Work Together*. Animal Teamwork. New York: PowerKids Press, 2018.

WEBSITES

Gorilla
animals.sandiegozoo.org/animals/gorilla

Gorilla | AMAZING ANIMALS
www.youtube.com/watch?v=rHhSCO5-3Pg

Mountain Gorilla
kids.nationalgeographic.com/animals/mountain-gorilla/

INDEX